Divinity...

A collection of poems

MONICA BHASIN

RedPenguin
BOOKS

Divinity
Copyright © 2022 Monica Bhasin

Photography by Jessica Ambats

Published by Red Penguin Books
Bellerose Village, New York
Library of Congress Control Number: 2022920133
ISBN
Print 978-1-63777-327-7

Contents

1. Divinity

2. The Beacon

3. The Calling

4. The Ally within

5. Your Inheritance

6. The Cure

7. The Trail

8. Reflections

9. Closer to you

10. Kindness

11. Free will

12. The Inevitable

13. Commonality

14. The Messenger and the Pilgrim

15. No more war (I will not fight)

16. Blue Sky

17. The Wishful plane

18. Ode to Long Island Sound

19. The Ordinary

20. The Time Traveler

21. Last Twilight

22. Alike

23. Anthem

24. The Approach

25. The Finish Line I

26. The Finish Line II

27. The Author

Divinity

We were divine long before we began the quest for divination
It was seeded into our beings when began the story of creation

If we listen carefully we would never need to be told
Love is inherent, compassion resides in our soul

It was coded in our genes and we never have to be taught
how to be kind without a second thought

Blindly do we stumble when we let it get out of our sight
when we forget who we truly are, the divine beings of light

Never are we higher then when we descend so low
When the descent is to lift others up, be it a friend or a foe

If we allow ourselves to feel then we truly will know
Divinity was always in us, our heart was its home

The Beacon

Lost over the stormy sea one dark winter's night
The little plane was losing hope, no land was in sight
And then suddenly there it was, that beacon of light
That angel in the dark, the savior of his life

He fought the gusty winds tossing him around
Guided by the Beacon, he touched steady ground
And then he felt gratitude, a feeling so profound
Thankful indeed he was to be alive, safe and sound

And so to the Beacon on the tower he then spoke
You who rescued me when there was no hope
What is my debt, how do I repay you
What do you want in return, tell me what can I do?

The Beacon on the tower smiled and glowed brighter
Surely I brought you in but all along you were the fighter
And repay me you shall when you share my light
Go be the Beacon and guide someone on a stormy night

The Calling

It rose from the mountains, it traveled with the drafts
Cutting through the cold winter air, it enveloped my craft

Travel with me it said, to the highest mountain peak
There you will find the answers to all that you seek

Maneuvering through the terrain I reached that summit
Hovered a while trying to ground my feet

There in a mountainous craven I settled down
In anticipation of what now would be found

For here it would be revealed, here I would see
Who sits there in the craven opposite to me

Who decides my fate, who writes my destiny
Who conjures up these twists and turns in my story

No mirage no illusion but how could it be
I was looking at myself, it was only me.

The Ally within

I know no boundaries, so I never come and go
I reside within you and conform to no shape or form that you know
I know no borders, but I surface when you need me the most
You may know me as that which stops you from being at your worst

I speak not, yet I am the voice that resonates deep within you
I am your conscience and often I guide you what to do
You know I am here when something in you tells you it is so
It's then when the line between right and wrong you begin to know

And often it isn't easy when the boundaries starts to fade
When black and white blurs up together and become just a shade
But if you don't subdue my voice, if you don't bury me so deep
We can work it out together, We can work it out as a team

Step back a little then and hear me speak to you
It's a battle and sometimes I can tell you what to do
And when you are at a crossroad and don't know which way to go
Listen for me in the stillness and I will surely let you know

Your Inheritance

This is your inheritance and you can make a fortune out of it
The breath of life that flows from your head to your feet
It's a gift of a lifetime and it's for you to redeem
This is your inheritance and this is where it begins

A magnificent physical body and a strong beating heart
What you do with it in this lifetime, is how long it will last
You will know this if you live long enough to tell
Your body is your inheritance so treat it really well

A powerhouse of possibilities, its the potential of your brain
The more you use and learn, the more it retains
A precious gift that if used very well
Will leave behind tales for generations to tell

Priceless are the gifts of your body and mind but the greatest gift of all
Is that inherent divine spark that's dormant in your soul
Light it up, love and be loved and then you will see
You will have inherited the world just as it was meant to be

The Cure

These were perilous times and in a land up North there was a cure
The exact coordinates of that place, no one knew for sure
It was said to be nestled in a valley between two mountain slopes
As the little plane set out to find the cure, he was filled with hope

For in a little village he called home a mysterious ailment had taken control
Robbing precious lives and bringing fear and dread to every soul
And the cure was in a potent herb in a land far away and so it was told
It was not a task for the weak, one victorious would be enduring and bold

He was summoned by the Captain as he prepared to depart
Watch out for three things, little plane, from the moment that you start

It will be an arduous journey full of risks and with an unpredictable outcome
Temptations will try and lure you away from your goal at every turn
Sole judgement you will have to make, unlike any that you may know
You alone will have to decide right from wrong and which way to go

Be it an arduous journey, said the little plane and may temptations lure
No matter the perils and dilemma I will return home with the cure

As he embarked on the journey, the deceptively calm winds on the first day
were replaced by erratic updrafts and downdrafts that threatened to blow him away
One strong gust of wind propelled him downwards towards a deadly descent
then another gently lifted him up bringing an end to the turbulence

As he aligned himself back on course, he whispered to the West Wind
I triumphed through challenges and all the tribulations that it brings
An arduous journey has it been but the perils I have been able to evade
Go tell the Captain I am still here because of my faith

He navigated by the North Star when his instruments broke
And reached the valley with the cure of which people spoke
Never had he seen a land so enchanting and mesmerizing as this
It was as close to Heaven as one could wish

As he smoothly glided into this land where the cure was known to be
He was heartily welcomed by the vibrant colorful flowers of the valley
As he toured around he was told that his home here he could make
But if he ever left the valley there was nothing with him that he could take

A dilemma indeed but he was certain it could be addressed later
He was sure that the rules could be changed for something that truly mattered
As he wandered through the valley he wondered why would he ever want to leave
For this land had everything and much more than one could need

The days were bright and sunny, comforting and warm were the nights
He prayed for strength when he saw his objectives disappear from his sight
And in the stillness of a beautiful morning he heard a voice speak
It's time for you to leave, remember the promises you have to keep

So then he spoke out aloud about his ailing village and all that was at stake
Precious lives could be saved if only the cure they would let him take
He pleaded with them with his heart and his soul and when it was time to go
He said he would seek the cure elsewhere if their answer was still a no

For he could not take what was not his, no matter what was at stake
The cure belonged to the valley, and it was not for him to take
As he bid farewell he was gifted a bouquet of flowers from the valley
And nestled in its center was the cure, his plea had been granted favorably

As he headed home he whispered to the West Wind, here's what I learnt
I made a judgment and a kind judgment was made for me in return
In times of weakness I prayed for help and it vanquished the lure
Go tell the Captain, said the little plane, I am coming home with the cure.

The Trail

Like magic there were rainbows in the clouds
Multiple rainbows and the more I looked the more I found
They were unlike any I had seen from down below on the ground

They were laid out in a pattern, they seemed to form a trail
Enchanted I followed them and they lead me right though a cloud veil

And then I found myself stationed in thin air
The sheer physicality of it no longer familiar

The magic continued to flow in this new realm I had found
It was euphoric, there was peace and contentment all around

This would be my new home, this is where I would stay
Even before I uttered those words I heard someone say

Answer these questions and then we will all know
If you belong here or back to where you came from you must go

Can you give selflessly and not expect to receive,
And to those who did you wrong can you truly forgive?

Unconditionally can you love one and all,
Can you take out the time to steady those who fall?

Can you stand up for the weak and defenseless,
Stay true to your convictions and not trade them all?

And to save a life can you give your life if that's what it takes,
In the face of adversity can you still stay in faith?

Purposefully I glided past the cloud veil and took back the trail
I knew I would keep trying no matter how many times I failed

And I would keep trying for the rest of my days
One day I would return when all those answers would be a Yes.

Reflections

In all of our existence, in all the time that we have been
Not all has been pleasant, not all the sights we have seen
We have known grace and love, enlightened beings of the light
Just as we have known darkness, and the unkind souls of the night

But in all that we see, it is only that what we choose to absorb
That radiates back from us, it reflects itself back multi fold
What we choose to see and retain mirrors back in our deeds
So choose wisely the sights that to your soul you will feed

Not everything that you see is fair and just, but don't let it change
Who you are and who you become, hold on to your faith
When you shutter out the darkness only your light will remain
And all its attempts to cloud your thoughts will be in vain

Blessed with free will, you alone can make that choice
To follow in the footsteps of enlightened beings and echo their voice
The treasure trove of wisdom that they left behind for you to absorb
will gracefully reflect in your actions of compassion and love

Reflect out your dreams the pure intentions of your thoughts
Let it resonate and amplify, you will see it redeem as it projects itself out
And reflect back an image of that familiar being you once knew
Even though the world is frowning she always smiled back at you

Closer to You

Closer to you, Sun, when you set,
then when you so gloriously rise in the eastern sky
For at dusk, as darkness crept,
I knew compassion as I thought you died

Closer to you, Nature, when I felt your raw scars,
when you were robbed and bared of your trees
As men waged on you his evil wars
even though you cried for peace

And so close to you, Child, when you fell
and hurt yourself and cried
For as I held you and prayed for your wounds to heal
understanding Him I tried

I was so close to you, Mother, when the storm came
When you grieved and in your tears were drowning
And as I strove to understand His ways
I realized, He wants you through pain to keep on learning

And close to you, Sister, when your wings broke
As you tried to fly higher then He intended
Let no tears be shed, were the words I spoke
Let her seek me through her grief that's what He told

Closer to you, Friend, when your end seemed so near
and your dreams died a cruel death.
As I held your hand and wiped your tears
closer to Him I felt.

Closer to myself, I feel when I can
Help those around me and care
Even in my small domain
For men must learn to stand by men
All through their grief, tears and pain

And so, God, I am closest to you when
In my simple ordinary way I can
Hold a hand, wipe a tear, it's only then
I realize your purpose for men

Kindness

Kindness is not kindness when it is expected back in kind
It is a word, a gesture or a deed, with no expectations in mind
It is a spontaneous action, well executed and then, well left behind
No expectations and nothing in return that you try to find

And so to those in their darkest moments, tell them what they should know
That behind the clouds and their darkness, a bright and guiding light glows
Sure as the sun sets and rises, the new morning that dawns will show
They are cherished and loved, never were they forgotten or alone

Kindness is contagious and even though it is not expected back in return
It propagates itself as the recipient observes, notes and learns
With one act of kindness a broken relationship you can mend
With one kind gesture your enemy can become your friend

A word of encouragement, a pat on the back or just a simple smile
Can uplift a tired soul and help them complete that last remaining mile
A life can be preserved when you show them that they are worthwhile
Every life has a meaning, everyone has a purpose and nothing is futile

In the end kindness finds a way to come back right where it started from
After being transferred around it finds its way back home
Practice kindness towards others and be kind to your own selves too
For often we are unkind to ourselves and that cannot be overlooked

Free Will

When fate conspires and everything seems to go downhill
Have faith in the ability of your free will.
When you aspire and they say it isn't meant to be
and so what if they say it isn't in your destiny?
Heavens relent, Fate reverses and Destiny rewrites
when you stand strong and never give up that fight.

The Inevitable

We are but victims of our own making
the unwitting fools of our concessions.
We are the subjugated aliases of our naming
defined by a lack of explanation.

And so we reconcile and we harmonize
condemning ourselves to eternal damnation.
Citing destiny we try and rationalize
and await the last moment to find salvation.

Blame not, then the inevitable
Say not, then what's to be shall be.
Know now, that it is free will that is capable
of ensuring that what now is will no longer be.

Commonality

You are not just a drop in the ocean or just one of the masses
Neither are you just one more face amongst these countless faces
You cannot let ties-downs and restraints lock you to a place
There are miles to cover, so one day you will break free from these chains

Each of us are distinct, we are defined by our own unique ability
But love is the common denominator, compassion is our commonality
We each have different experiences as varied as the paths that we take
But we share a common destiny for our collective purpose is the same

For each of us a day will dawn when the winds will be just right
then our tie-downs will break and propel us into flight
As we soar higher and higher, we must nurture the thoughts on our minds
Thoughts of our brothers and sisters, the masses that we leave behind

When the awakening dawns, it will be like a thunderbolt in the sky
Then we will see it clearly and understand all the reasons why
It is in our commonality that we are tightly bound
It is in our brotherhood that our purpose will be found.

Part 1: The Messenger

He was on a mission, he flew from here to there
There was this word of God that he wanted to share
And the word of God that he tried so hard to seed
Was so simple in its terms that not one soul paid heed

Yet they paused, curious to hear what he had to say
Then bemused at his earnestness, they went about their way
For they had heard it all countless times before
It had been repeated so often, it was just easy to ignore

The Messenger continued on, relentless in his quest
Relaying his message just as he knew best
And he pleaded to the people, practice what you know
In your daily lives let your love and kindness show

Part 2: The Pilgrim

A brilliant scholar, at a young age he mastered Theology
And now in a theorem he planned to map universal logic
So he deciphered religious verses and decoded ancient relics
Strategically he aligned them with quantum mechanics

But in one desperate moment he realized that it was all an illusion
For no matter how hard he tried he could deduce no conclusion
Fearing insanity he abandoned all logic and reason
And told himself that when the time was right, it would appear in his vision

And thus he became The Pilgrim, still seeking out the source
Simple little answers that would put him back on course
And when the time was right, in his vision appeared The Messenger
And in his simple little message was The Pilgrims answer.

No more war (I will not fight)

The war sirens were blaring on, for each side thought that they were right
There would be no further negotiations, now was the time to fight
So the ground troops armored up and deployed to strategic positions
And the air fleet prepared to bombard enemy targets in their vision

The Generals were hard at work with strategies and a battle plan
As gradually into the enemy territory their troops would advance
The air and the ground troops were brimming with anticipation
For they felt like true patriots who would die fighting for their nation

And thus began the destructive air raids and fatal ground combats
Men against Men, Brother against Brother, sunrise to sunset
While the leaders and warlords mulled over the next certain checkmate
Many of their troops fell, succumbing to a precarious fate

Those majestic buildings which took decades to build
Now collapsed to the ground, part of the dusty battlefield
And innocent lives were lost in that war ravaged land
When the ravages of war they no longer could withstand

As the ground troops advanced though a desolate city street
One of the men tarried behind trying to rest his weary feet
He surveyed the destruction around him of life and of matter
And wondered if he stopped now, would he be called a traitor

Amongst the battle weary troops, a single thought was on every mind,
This doesn't feel right, it's not my battle and I do not want to fight.
War is not the answer, this can't be the right way
And they wondered who amongst them would be the first to say

Up in the sky, the air fleet felt very accomplished
Not a single target in their vision had they missed
But their hearts weighed heavy even though it was a certain victory
As they reloaded their missiles and headed towards the next city

Static was on their radios with what was a muffled up sound
It strangely sounded like chanting and it was coming from the ground
They descended rapidly below in a controlled flight
To get a better glimpse of a rather peculiar sight

The ground troops were sitting down in perfect straight files
Chanting with their arms crossed and their guns by their side
Who started the first chant no one really knew or cared
For to chant that collective thought they were no longer scared

This is not my battle, I will not fight,
No more war, let's make this right
And there it was, that one collective thought
It had whirled around and echoed to a shout

Stronger by the minute, the chant rose up several thousand feet
And the air fleet cared no more about victory or defeat
They joined the chant and it reverberated in the air
Rejoicing in the knowledge that the end of the battle was near.

Blue Sky

Sunny new day and a crisp winter morning
The air is still pure and the day has a meaning
We can marvel at the beauty of it all and the amazing blue sky
But can we share this with the next generation to come by?

Oh what a shame it would be to let it all go
To lose this to a time when the clouds will always be low
For when the smog, the haze, the polluted air no longer can we take
We will lose it all to this one big mistake, we were just too late

There is always a choice, a path to take
Our future is paved by the decisions we make
We will know if we contemplate and take a closer look
Where we are today is the consequence of the actions that we took

So let's pay attention, let's heed the sounds
No longer subtle are the crumbling signs all around
How hard is it to comprehend what lack of foresight does
Don't let the beauty end here, don't let it die with us.

The Wishful Plane

I am bright and shiny, Captain, said he
I would like to join your fleet, if you would please let me.
I see your troops fly by and oh, what a marvelous sight
I could fly just as well and if you give me a chance, I just might

But the wishful plane knew that he just wasn't their kind
He was different with a rather unusual bent of mind
He had a mind of his own and even though he was bright
In his quest for perfection, he couldn't follow instructions right

It won't be easy, said the Captain, for you have much to learn
It might be a while before a rank in my fleet you can earn
So learn and practice, try your best and then let me know
If you think you are ready to join my show

So the little plane lifted himself up, he tried and he tried
Until he could no more and then he broke down and cried
For in spite of all his best efforts, he could never get it just right
He was trying so hard to make each one a perfect flight

Little plane, said the Captain, don't lose that smile
And let me tell you something worth a while
Persevere and know that you have all that it takes
Don't stop trying, for giving up can be the only mistake

Failure is temporary and the only certainty that will prevail
is that you kept trying no matter how many times you failed
For in the end, it won't matter whether you fail or succeed
if you never stopped trying, you were already one of my fleet

Ode to Long Island Sound

The gleaming glistening still waters of Long Island Sound
Reflect the blue hues of the skies above and all around

The tiny white waves playfully hug the shoreline
In rapport with the sandy banks reflecting the sunshine

The gentle turns of the sandy beaches in all its simplicity
merges with the rocky coastline embracing its diversity

And in the deep grey waters, the barges trudge along faithfully
Steadfast and strong they move along purposefully

The ripples across the water that can be seen occasionally
are from vessels transporting revelers celebrating life and the living

The ebb and flow of life continues on even though still the waters may seem
In its stillness it reflects the transient nature of everything.

The vibrant water colors, multiples shades of green and blue
Ever changing, from every angle, they present a different point of view

And one glorious sunny day over these deep still waters
The little plane took into perspective life and what truly matters

She smiled as she raised her nose ever so slightly for a kiss from the sun
And the sun smiled back when his rays bounced off her wings in the turn

Perfection came about that day when perfect she no longer tried to be
It was in flight, over Long Island Sound, flying effortlessly

The Ordinary

On a beautiful sunny day when the weather was just sublime
The little plane was flying around having a marvelous time
He rocked his wings at the tiny clouds scurrying by
What a wonderful day it was to be there, just to be alive

As evening fell he headed back and when he came to a rest
He was introduced to a few of the finest and the very best
He was truly amazed at how perfect they all were
With great interest he listened to everything they each had to share

I carry cargo and supplies, said the Cargo plane, I fly far across gigantic seas
And the Fighter plane said, I protect my land from its enemies
I rescue the lost and troubled for I am the Rescue plane
I have learnt my trade well, added the Training plane, so now I teach and train
Expert at maneuvers, said the Aerobatic plane, I entertain and delight
and the Passenger plane said, I connect people through my flight

And they kindly asked him what had he done through the day
What was his purpose, in a few words if he could say
The little plane fell silent, no words came to his mind
No discernible purpose to his existence he could find

A wise old plane in the corner from a time long ago
said to the little plane, I can tell you what you need to know

You touched someone's life and they touched yours
you gave joy to others and your own life you enjoyed
In your daily life you have continued to live faithfully
That's the reason for your existence, don't you see?
Not all are masters and experts, not all are extraordinary
Sometimes your purpose is to just be there, it's just to be

The Time Traveler

In one of his sojourns, the little plane made an acquaintance
With a strange looking craft erratically hovering in the distance
It was the Time Traveler and he had so much to say
To the curious little plane he had encountered on his way

I am an observer, said the Time Traveler, recording history is all I do
I cannot intervene even though there so many times I would like to
And so I travel through time and I record what I see
I try to be an impartial observer but it's not always easy

I have witnessed the folly of mankind and the senseless wars that they wage
Unending disputes over boundaries that they so foolishly rage
The deep seated scars, these casualties of life and destruction of land
are the consequences of war that cannot justify the outcome in the end

And I bear witness to the progress of mankind and the civilizations forward
Their progress I found is proportional to their respect for Mother Earth
When they drain her callously of her resources they have faced her wrath
Partnering in harmony they have thrived in her warmth

I have traveled through centuries and I have seen them come and go
And every once in a while I meet that someone who engages my soul
These are the beings who give when they have so little of their own
Who share the love and kindness that they themselves have never known

And then there are those who are trapped in the illusion of their lifetimes
In self-gratification they think their answers they will find
And so that is how they live from one life to the next
Unaware that they have failed yet another test.

Time after time the same foolish decisions people make
If they don't learn or correct, they will have to re-live every mistake.
It would be so much easier if they knew there is no escape
Unresolved issues will still be here every time they wake.

And you, little plane, said the Time Traveler, you and I have met before
But what was in the past is history now, so ponder over it no more
What is recorded ahead will be dictated by the path that you now take
Live well in the present for that's how history will be made

Last Twilight

Centuries ago when over the mountain cliffs we met
Remember then, to me what you said
Legends we would make, barriers we would break
we would conquer time and vanquish space

Truly of great magnitude, our flights were one of a kind
Perfect formations, the unison of soul, body and mind.

But one day we fell and we lost our way
I succumbed to the night, you to the day
Destined there on to meet at twilight but never to stay

Then we were two black ravens, you and I
In the sweltering heat of the Grand Canyons we would fly
Below me the red river, above you the blue sky

And in the war zones we were first of the crew
Across the bloodied battlefield on opposite sides we flew
Fleeting encounters at twilights yet we never knew

Time and space recycled countless times since and so did we
We met at every twilight yet never did we see

And one day when space was colonized
In a strange habitat where there was neither day nor night
There we found ourselves face to face
Finally we had conquered time and vanquished space.

Alike

A vast ocean separates the two continents on which we each took our first breath
Born to different parents of a different race we have inherited different physical traits
But we were born the same way and we shared the same Father till we came to be
We are not different if we share the same legacy

Our clumsy baby steps and the tears when we fell and hurt ourselves so many times
But if we were held, comforted and loved then it was all fine
And for all our needs we cried and cried till someone came
We are not different if our need to be nurtured is the same

Our first loves with the ones that we believed in and hoped were true
We shared the same excitement of something special and new
If the same love that we gave and in return tried so hard to find
How then can your first love story be so different from mine?

And the heartache and the pain that followed when we learnt
That our true loves weren't true and that we no longer could trust
It seemed that the world had ended and we wouldn't live another day
How then can we be different if we hurt and cry the same way?

We wake up to the same glorious sun, the one which rises every morning
We welcome yet another day, a blessed new chance to continue living
And we hope to find love and be truly loved, impossible though it may seem
We are not very different in the childlike way we hope and dream

We delight in the beauty of this world, the first raindrops and the April showers
The beautiful mountains, the streams and the colorful fragrant flowers
We share happiness and gratitude for all the joys that each new day brings
We are very similar in the way we laugh and smile and enjoy the same things

The same pale moon that we look up at, is looking down at us too
It makes me question my purpose and my existence, just as it does to you
We share the realization that we are but a tiny speck in this infinite space
We are alike in how we question and try to find our own individual place

There were moments in life when we found ourselves in deep despair
No one seemed to understand why we struggled with darkness and fear
In those moments we turned to the same heavenly Father and we prayed
We are not different at all if we both believe and have faith

We lived through most of our existence doing the best that we could do
We kept our faith and belief alive even though our purpose we never really knew
And we will share our experiences in a beautiful land one fine day
We will truly know how alike we are when we arrive there the same way

Anthem

On a bright and crisp winter morning the little plane started out early
He was all fueled up, ready to go and resonating with the sun's energy
He hummed a happy little tune as he prepared for his flight
For he was doing what he loved most and the weather was just right

Heading up North he floated effortlessly over a captivating landscape
Much like a dream, the one from which one would rather not wake
In perfect harmony with the landscape he was so deeply immersed
So much a part of his surroundings that he felt one with the universe

And in that blissful moment, words came flooding into his memory
The words that his Captain said to him when he first started his journey
It's difficult out there and I understand why you don't want to go
But go you must, to fulfill your purpose and to find a way to grow

And while you are out there, adopt this anthem, a creed to live by
It is not easy, little plane, but you must give it your best try

Hard work is not optional, it is an absolute necessity
It is only a dedicated effort that will turn your dreams into a reality
Don't let daily routine weigh you down as just one more strife
a well-practiced approach will help you in all your successful flights

Knowledge is power so always observe, note and learn
Then you will find that the winds are in your favor, you will see them return
Humility is most essential, it will broaden your horizons as you grow
And it's okay to admit that there is still a lot that you don't know

Courage in times of adversity will help you overcome an obstacle
Never give up, a determined approach will make turbulence easy to handle
Make decisions by carefully examining the pros and cons
Any finally favor what is right even if for you it may seem wrong

Patience is necessary so don't rush and divert out of course
You will arrive safely at your destination even though it may seem slow
With full attention focus on your tasks and stop looking for the prize
Then your flightpath will be reduced to half and the destination will appear in sight

But in spite of it all if you ever lose control and can't go on, reach out to me
I will lift you up for I am always by your side even if you can't see
These words, Captain, said the little plane, are not always in my memory
Yet I abide by them for they are unconsciously embedded in me

For the times when I was lost and a path to navigate I was trying to find
I was guided through this anthem that emerged from the recesses of my mind
And for those doubtful moments, I see now what then I did not see
That even when I don't remember you, you never forget me

The Approach

It had been a long day as the little plane settled down for the night
Tomorrow would be another day, one more leg to cover on his flight
Right from the start, the journey he had agreed upon had been difficult
He had worked hard to get by and he never seemed to have any luck

Though firmly stationed on the ground, he wasn't inclined to trust
Any time now, he thought, this treacherous wind will turn into a gust
It had been a tiresome day and he was feeling rather sorry for himself
It was quite unusual for he usually handled adversities very well

The Captain assessed the situation and decided it was time
To intervene and curb these thoughts while they were still benign
Recall your training, said the Captain, for you have let it get out of sight
If you had followed my instructions, this would not be your plight

The little plane decided to air his grievances and he had plenty to say
He started with the weather and why the winds never blew his way
The clouds seemed to show up everywhere that he looked
And turbulence was on every flight path no matter which one he took

And about good luck, he knew others who had plenty
It seemed like he had been forgotten for he didn't have any
He had shared his resources even though he did not have a lot
But he never got anything in return, it seemed that everyone just forgot

He had navigated through thunderstorms but he never had a guide
It would have been nice to know had someone been on his side
The first leg of the journey was over but it had taken so very long
And the worst part was that he didn't know if he had done something wrong

I have your answers, said the Captain to the little plane
There are times when we all need to relearn and get retrained
All your answers are in one place, they all have the same source
It's all about how you look at it, it's all about your approach

If you did the ground work well and laid the foundation right
Perhaps you could have had good weather throughout your flight
And for unexpected thunderstorms and dark clouds that often roll
Just put in your best effort and do what you must to remain in control

About good luck, rely on hard work instead and even though it doesn't seem fair
Have faith in the universe that one day you will be granted your share
You shared your resources with those in need, but what you must learn
Is that you never really shared anything if you expected it back in return

Share your experiences, perhaps there's someone that you could guide
Perhaps someone could learn from your mistakes and have a better ride
The first leg was very long because you were focused on the prize
You forgot to enjoy the simple little things and have a pleasant flight

The second leg of the flight would soon begin and it would be the best one yet
For the little plane would practice his training, this time he would not forget
Tomorrow would be another day but it wouldn't be just another flight
It would be the best one yet for he was all prepared to get this one right

The Finish Line 1

Even though it was not a race, he was very well prepared
He had laid out a foundation early on, his path-to victory was made
Religiously had he lived thus so far, staying true to his beliefs
It came easy to him, for he had nothing to take but much to give

Each new day was a miracle as he learnt more and more
Each year found him better, so much wiser than before
Often he made judgement on others though he knew it wasn't right
But it's quite all right, he thought, being that this was his only vice

And judge often he did, in particular one of his Arch Nemesis
Defining and categorizing him, based on their profound differences
He often judged him with sadness and a lot more with pity
For this one had lost his ways and eye to eye they could not see

Throughout life their paths frequently crossed
And each time his Arch nemesis at him verbally lashed.
He felt offended each time and with the words hurting deep inside
he found it difficult to forgive his Arch nemesis even though he tried

In bitter moments he told himself to keep the finish line in sight
Victorious would be only one, the only one who was right
Across the finish line he knew they each would find their place
And he was certain of the fact that they would not share the same space

His final steps toward the finish line were firm and steady
He had prepared for this all his life and was more than ready
Meanwhile his Arch Nemesis was stumbling towards the finish line
With much fear and apprehension of what was waiting there for him to find

One step short of the finish line and he felt that he could not go on
He would not feel victorious even though he could have won
And so he turned back and held out his arms towards the one left behind
He gently lifted his Arch Nemesis and together they crossed the finish line

And then, it mattered no more who and what was right or wrong
Across the finish line there was only love and nothing more
Absolute unity, nothing to leave behind and none to save
All one, the lion and the lamb, the sinner and the saint

The Finish Line II

He convinced himself early on in life that this is how things ought to be
There was just this one life and he would live it to its prime and glory
If he got what he wanted at any cost it could only mean that he was strong
Even if he got there by stepping over others it wasn't all that wrong

So he breezed through life with much comfort and ease
It came easy to him because he didn't allow his inner voice to speak
He subdued it while keeping his needs above everyone else
And told himself that everyone was responsible for their own self

His disregard for others reflected strongly towards his Arch Nemesis
That holier than thou preacher who lived down the street
Whose compassion and kindness disturbed his mind
A reasonable explanation for which he could not find

Seasons changed, the years rolled by and then came that fateful day
When he had taken all that he could and now it was time to pay
He found himself stumbling towards the finish line scared and lonely
His fair weather friends had fled and there were none to hold him steady

And he looked back at his self-indulgent life, a life not well lived
A life not well lived for it was all about taking with nothing to give
Nothing could he take now, all of his possessions would be left behind
What he could only take now, were the thoughts on his mind

Then he heard a voice call his name and felt himself gently lifted up
His Arch Nemesis had arrived and showered him with compassion and love
Nothing else was needed, nothing else that could heal his soul
Except the reassurance that he was loved and part of the whole

And in his darkest moment, the one that found him broken and scared
He realized now what it felt like when someone showed that they cared
As he moved past the finish line he was engulfed in a bright light
There would be another chance and this time he would get it right

The Author

The Author of our story, in reverence we stand before thee.
Our name on a blank page, it was the first chapter of the story.
We see the years roll by as in the chapters as per your itinerary.
It's your outline, our free will and together we will complete this journey.

We revel, rejoice and celebrate each milestone, each one that we have lived
and hope to make it the best, the next milestone that we have yet to reach.
Our destination may have been written but we can choose the course
and change the outcome in our favor if we have the right approach.

And so through dark clouds and tempestuous skies when we do glide,
it is with faith for we know you are always by our side.
Throughout our journey we remain ever so cognizant of your role.
Though we fly our crafts, you are in control.
We of our crafts, and you of our souls.

www.ingramcontent.com/pod-product-compliance
Lightning Source LLC
Chambersburg PA
CBRC101827090426
42811CB00023B/1918